THE ME I'M LEARNING TO BE

REVISED EDITION

by Imogene Forte

Incentive Publications, Inc.
Nashville, Tennessee

Illustrated by Susan Eaddy
Cover by Becky Cutler
Edited by Sherri Y. Lewis

ISBN 0-86530-061-5

TABLE OF CONTENTS

There's more to me than meets the eye,
I'm beginning to understand.
It's what I think and how I feel
That make me what I am.

Why do I do the things I do
And say the things I say?
What is important, and how do I tell?
I'm learning more each day.

I learn from friends and family,
From work, from play, from school.
I've also learned to take some time
To sit and think things through.

The more I learn, the more I grow,
And then the more I see
Just how much more I want to know
The Me I'm Learning To Be!

A NEW YEAR

On the first day of a new school year:

1. I can hardly wait to _____
   _____
   _____
   _____
   _____ .

2. I hope my schedule is _____
   _____
   _____
   _____ .

3. The extracurricular activity that I hope to participate in is _____
   _____
   _____ .

4. I wish the principal would _____
   _____ .

5. I hope my teacher will _____
   _____ .

6. I look forward to _____
   _____ .

7. I dread _____
   _____ .

8. I hope to make improvement this year in _____
   _____ .

9. When I think of homework, I _____
   _____ .

10. More than anything else, I wish _____
    _____ .

Name _____

FEELINGS

Complete these sentences to describe feelings you have had.

1. I felt proud when _____

_____

_____

_____

_____.

2. I remember feeling very humble when _____

_____

_____.

3. I felt very sad when _____

_____

_____.

4. I wanted to shout with happiness when _____

_____.

5. I thought I would cry when _____

_____.

6. My heart began to pound with fear when _____

_____.

7. I was discouraged by _____

_____.

8. My gratitude was overflowing when _____

_____.

9. I was so embarrassed I wanted to hide my head when _____

_____.

10. I could hardly believe my good luck when _____

_____.

Name _____

FRIENDLY FEELINGS

Ask a friend to play this game with you.

START

Rules:

1. The first player writes a word that names a way good friends should feel about each other. One letter must fit into each square. The player circles the last letter of the word and writes his or her initials there.

2. The second player thinks of a "friendly feeling" word that begins with the circled letter and writes it in the following squares, circling the last letter and placing his or her initials there. The game continues until all the squares are filled or neither player can think of another word.

3. Each filled square counts one point. The player with the highest score wins the game. (Players will want to write long words as they are worth more points.)

4. To get started, you might want to use one of these: trusting, thoughtful, kind.

5. Just for fun, turn the game around and play it with "unfriendly feeling" words.

Name _____

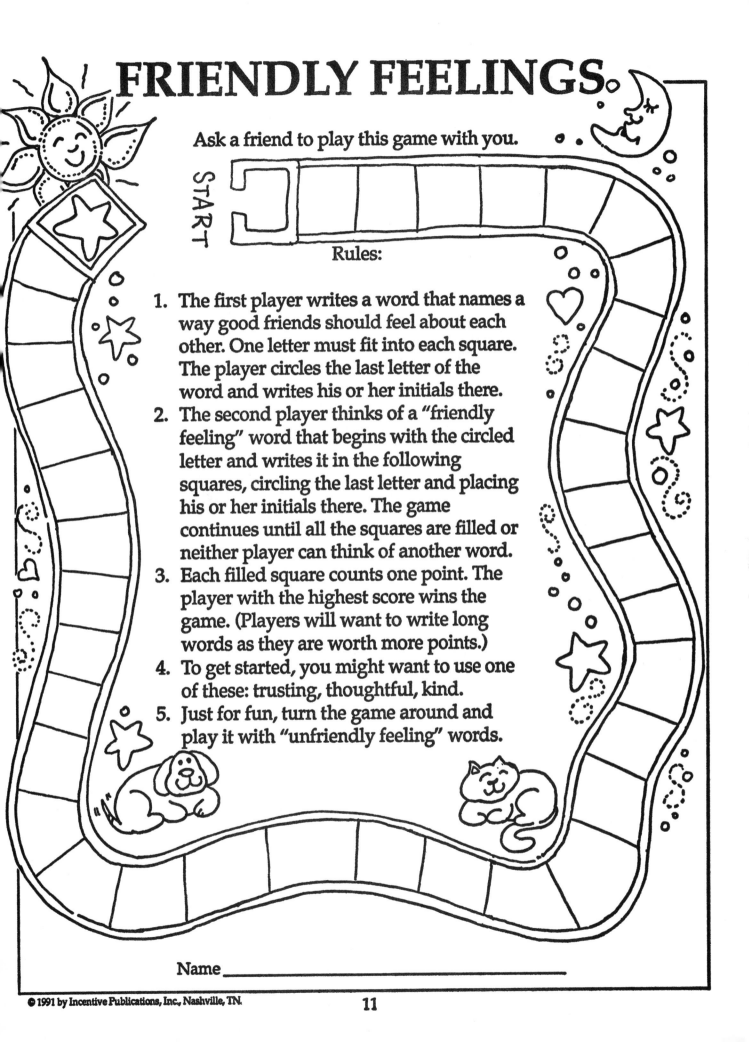

A WORD ON FEELINGS

Write just one word to tell how **you** would feel in each of the situations.

You are nominated for **class president.** You win the election by **receiving almost** all the votes. _____

OR

You win the election by **receiving only** one vote more than the **person who ran** against you. _____

You leave your seat during work time to help a friend who **does not** understand a math problem. In a cross voice, the teacher **asks you to** return to your seat immediately. _____

OR

When the friend asks you for help, you say that **you are not supposed to** talk during free time, and you continue with **your own work.**

_____

On a hot summer day, your friends kick off their **shoes to wade in a pool** marked with a sign: ABSOLUTELY NO TRESPASSING. **You decide not** to wade even though you want to very much. _____

OR

You kick off your shoes and wade in because **you do not want to be** "different." _____

Name _____

FEELINGS TO FIND

Find and circle the fifteen words below that name ways you have felt or may feel.

After all the words are found, color the "good" feelings red and the "bad" feelings green.

How many red words do you have? _____

How many green words do you have? _____

A	N	G	R	Y	O	L	A	H	E	G
U	P	S	E	T	R	G	A	L	D	E
J	F	E	A	R	F	U	L	F	U	N
O	E	D	H	U	R	T	I	P	M	E
Y	O	N	A	S	H	S	O	Y	B	R
F	R	U	S	T	R	A	T	E	D	O
U	K	J	K	I	N	D	T	A	F	U
L	O	V	I	N	G	E	S	I	E	S
U	R	E	N	G	P	A	L	O	N	E
N	A	N	X	I	O	U	S	R	A	G

Word List:

kind   angry   dumb
loving   upset   hating
alone   generous   sad
anxious   fearful
joyful   hurt
trusting   frustrated

Name _____

A LOST KITTEN CAUSES TROUBLE

Pierre was walking down his block after school when he saw a kitten. Pierre thought the kitten looked lost and lonely. He stopped to play with it and decided to take it home. He gave it some milk and left it in the yard.

The next day when Pierre came home from school, his mother was upset. She told Pierre that a lady had come for the kitten. The lady said that the kitten belonged to her little boy and that he had cried all night because his kitten was gone.

Was Pierre guilty of
- ☐ stealing?
- ☐ unkindness?
- ☐ thoughtlessness?

Write about the feelings you would have if you were Pierre.

_____

_____

_____

_____

If you were Pierre, what would you do about it?

_____

_____

_____

_____

_____

Name_____

CHANGES ON THE WAY

Carrie and Beth had been best friends since they had started to school. They lived on the same street and walked to school together every day. Their parents were friends, and the families took trips and spent a great deal of time together. At the beginning of the school year when the girls were entering sixth grade, Beth was told that because of her high test scores and good grades, she could advance to the seventh grade. The girls would no longer be able to spend time together during the school day.

Do you think Carrie and Beth will continue to be best friends? _____

Write a paragraph to tell how you would feel if you were Carrie.

_____

_____

_____

_____

_____

_____

_____

Write a paragraph to tell how you would feel if you were Beth.

_____

_____

_____

_____

_____

_____

_____

Name _____

FRIENDSHIP TREE

Circle ten words on the word tree that you would like for your friends to use to describe you.

Then write two sentences to tell what you would want your best friend to say about you.

Loyal
Determined

Generous
Creative
Agreeable   Friendly
Questioning
Sharing

Interesting
Ambitious
Strong
Inventive
Daring
Cheerful

Accepting
Pleasant
Witty
Considerate
Thoughtful

Brave
Kind

Dependable

_____
_____
_____
_____

Name _____

MEMORIES

Finish the sentences.

1. I'll always remember a time I felt happy because _____ _____ _____.

2. I'll always remember a time I felt sad because _____ _____ _____.

3. I'll always remember a time I felt afraid because _____ _____ _____.

4. I'll always remember a time I felt left out because _____ _____.

5. I'll always remember a time I felt strong because _____ _____.

6. I'll always remember a time I felt intelligent because _____ _____.

7. I'll always remember a time I felt successful because _____ _____.

8. I'll always remember a time I felt frustrated because _____ _____.

9. I'll always remember a time I felt so angry because _____ _____.

10. I'll always remember a time I felt so proud because _____ _____.

Name _____

RAINY DAY PROBLEMS

Barbara left her umbrella at her grandmother's house. The next day it rained. She borrowed her neighbor's umbrella to walk to the library. When she had checked out her books, the sun was shining and she forgot all about the umbrella. Barbara never thought of it again until a week later when the neighbor called and asked her to bring the umbrella back. When she returned to the library to get the umbrella, it was not there.

Was Barbara guilty of
□ irresponsibility?   □ dishonesty?   □ disobedience?

Write about the feelings you would have if you were Barbara.

_____

_____

_____

_____

If you were Barbara, what would you do about it?

_____

_____

_____

_____

_____

Name _____

MOVIE MADNESS

It was after ten o'clock, and Samantha's mother had told her twice to get ready for bed.

The movie Samantha was watching was almost over, and she really wanted to see the ending. So she ignored her mother and continued to sit in front of the TV.

Finally Samantha's father called from the other room and told her to go to bed immediately.

Frustrated and resentful, Samantha jumped up from the rocking chair. As she did, she knocked one of her mother's antique vases off the table and it shattered into pieces.

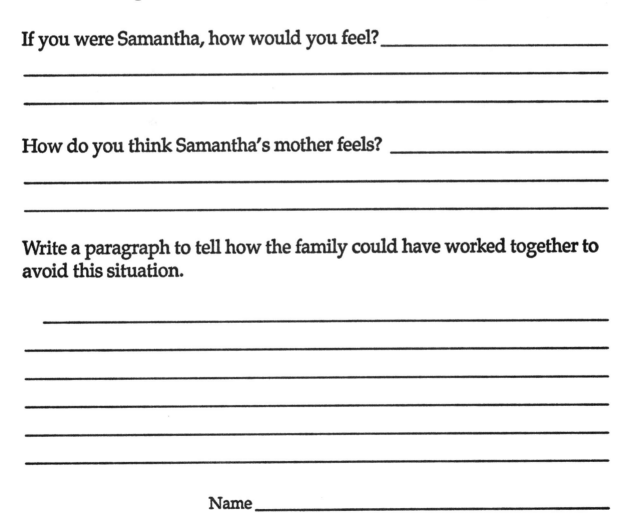

If you were Samantha, how would you feel? _____

_____

_____

How do you think Samantha's mother feels? _____

_____

_____

Write a paragraph to tell how the family could have worked together to avoid this situation.

_____

_____

_____

_____

_____

_____

_____

Name _____

LOOKING AHEAD

1. When I think about being old, I usually feel _____ _____ _____.

2. I think that being a child is _____ _____ _____ _____ than being old because _____ _____ _____.

3. Most of the old people I know are _____ _____ _____.

4. The thing I think the old people I know probably like most about me is _____ _____.

5. When I am old, I would like to be like _____ because _____.

6. When I am old, I hope I will not be _____ _____.

7. I am looking forward to being able to _____ and _____.

8. I hope people will say that I am a _____ _____ older person.

9. On the whole, I think that being old will be _____ _____.

Name _____

WHAT NEXT?

Write two or three sentences to tell what you would do next in each of these situations.

You and your best friend have agreed to meet after school to finish a relief map that is due for a social studies project tomorrow. At noon your friend tells you that he has decided to work on a project with someone else and that you can do whatever you want about the map. The unfinished map is at the friend's house, and he says the house is locked and no one will be home before 9 p.m.

_____

_____

_____

_____

_____

Your summer job is watering and weeding a neighbor's garden. The neighbor is out of town and will not return until the end of the summer. At first you are excited about the job and you want the money you are earning. As the summer wears on, however, you become more and more bored with the job. The garden is hot and sticky and full of creepy, crawly things. Part of you thinks, "Oh, well, I don't want this job again next summer anyway." Another part of you thinks, "But I promised to take good care of the garden."

_____

_____

_____

_____

_____

Name _____

I NEVER WOULD

You want what?!

1. I never would ask a friend to ____

_____

_____

because _____

_____

_____.

2. I never would expect my teacher to

_____

because _____

_____

_____.

3. I never would promise to _____
   because _____.

4. I never would want to be _____
   because _____.

5. I never would give away my _____
   because _____.

6. I never would tell my parents _____
   because _____.

7. I never would go _____
   because _____.

8. I never would write _____
   because _____.

9. I never would play with _____
   because _____.

10. I never would spend my money for _____
    because _____.

Name _____

I NEVER WOULD, BUT...

I know a man who said, "I never would *knowingly* hurt a person."

I know a girl who said, "I never would *purposely* tell a lie."

I know a boy who said, "I never would *plan* to cheat or steal."

I know a woman who said, "I never would *choose* to be unkind to animals."

I read about a great writer who said, "I never would *selfishly* put my career ahead of my family."

Think carefully before you complete each of the sentences below.

1. I never would *knowingly* _____

   but _____.

2. I never would *purposely* _____

   but _____.

3. I never would *plan* to _____

   but _____.

4. I never would *choose* to _____

   but _____.

5. I never would be *selfishly* _____

   but _____.

6. Of all the things I hope I never would do, I especially hope I never

   would _____

   because _____

   _____.

Name _____

SCENE OF THE CRIME

Andy and Bert were such good friends that when they each received money for Christmas, they decided to combine it and buy an electronic toy they could share.

As they were browsing through the electronics store looking at radios, CD players, and games, they noticed Pete – a boy from school – enter the store. Pete did not see them and walked quietly to a calculator display, picked up a small calculator, slipped it into his pocket, and left the store.

Write a good paragraph that tells what you would do if you were Andy or Bert.

_____
_____
_____
_____
_____
_____

Write another paragraph that tells what you think would happen next.

_____
_____
_____
_____
_____
_____

Name_____

NEW KID IN CLASS

Rose had been the new student in Ms. Brinkley's class for almost a month. No one had been friendly to her, even though she felt she had tried to be friendly. She was very lonely.

One day, Ms. Brinkley introduced another new student to the class. His name was Bobby. He was very short and very shy, and he blushed when Ms. Brinkley introduced him.

At recess, the three girls Rose most wanted to be her friends approached and began to make fun of Bobby. Here was Rose's chance to join in and be part of the group.

Write a paragraph that tells what you would do if you were Rose and what effect this action would have on Bobby.

_____

_____

_____

_____

_____

_____

_____

_____

_____

_____

_____

_____

_____

_____

Name _____

LEFT OUT

Meg and Sarah were best friends, and they always ate lunch together. Meg's class went to lunch first, so she saved Sarah a seat every day. One day Sarah got to the end of the lunch line and went toward their usual table. She was excited about telling Meg that Tommy, the smartest kid in school, had asked for help on a math assignment. But Meg wasn't there. Sarah looked around and saw Meg at another table. When Meg saw Sarah, she started laughing and whispering to two other girls. Sarah felt awful. There was no seat saved for her!

On the lines below, write what you would do if you were Sarah, what you think would happen next, and how you think Meg and Sarah's friendship would be affected.

Name _____

NO HIDING PLACE

When Patty's neighbors came back from Florida, they brought her a little live alligator. At school the next day, she told all her friends about her new pet, but no one would believe her.

"I do have a pet alligator," she insisted. "Just wait. I'll bring it tomorrow and show you."

"You can't bring live animals to school," they teased. "But if it's not alive, it'll be fine."

The next day, Patty hid the alligator in her lunch box and took it to school early. When her friends arrived in the classroom, Patty opened the lunch box and proudly showed off her pet. All the students ooohed and aaahed, but suddenly everyone was quiet.

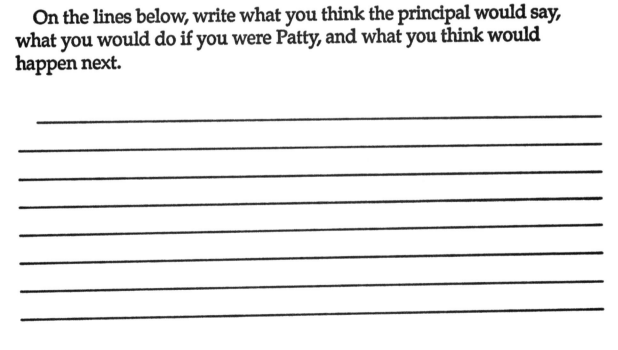

Patty looked up to see the principal staring down at her with a very stern face.

On the lines below, write what you think the principal would say, what you would do if you were Patty, and what you think would happen next.

_____

_____

_____

_____

_____

_____

_____

Name _____

TALENT SHOW

THE HOOFING HOLSTEINS

The teacher had announced that the annual talent show would be held at the end of the school year. David had started planning a dance routine with four friends. The group had picked out costumes and music and set up a practice schedule.

A week before the talent show, David suddenly remembered that he had promised to do some juggling tricks with Melissa, a girl he had been friendly with when she was new at school. It was too late to get a good act together in time for the show. Melissa hadn't mentioned it, but David felt sure that she remembered his promise and had not planned anything else.

If you were David...

Would you forget about it and go ahead with your routine? _____
_____
_____

Would you talk with Melissa and explain what happened? _____
_____
_____

What would you do? _____
_____
_____

Why? _____
_____
_____

Name _____

TOO LONG ON THE PHONE

"Oh, there you are, Dexter," said his father as he came into the room and saw Dexter on the phone. "I'm on my way to the Lodge meeting. Here's the phone number. Now get off the phone, do your homework, and keep Lottie out of trouble. I'll be back in about an hour."

"OK, Dad," said Dexter, but he went back to his phone conversation. He didn't hear 3-year-old Lottie sneak into the bathroom a few minutes later. She loved to close the drain, fill the tub, and sail her boats in it. Unfortunately, she didn't know how to turn off the water.

Dexter was still on the phone when his father came home, so he hung up quickly and started his homework. Suddenly he heard Lottie crying and his father yelling. He ran to the bathroom and saw water everywhere! His father turned to him angrily.

"Well," he snapped, "what do you have to say for yourself?"

On the lines below, write what you would do if you were Dexter and what you would expect to happen next.

_____

_____

_____

_____

_____

_____

_____

_____

_____

Name _____

DOUBLE TROUBLE

Sandy and Cathy's twin cousins Megan and Marcia were 2-years-old and a lot of fun to play with. One afternoon Sandy and Cathy were playing in the twins' bedroom while their parents were cooking dinner. Sandy was jumping on the bed with Megan when she lost control, and Megan fell and hit her head. After Megan stopped crying, Cathy said she was going to tell Megan's parents what had happened. Sandy began to cry because she was afraid Cathy would tell. Cathy insisted that Megan hit her head so hard that her parents should be told.

Write a paragraph to tell what you would do if you were Cathy and why.

_____

_____

_____

_____

_____

_____

_____

_____

_____

_____

_____

_____

Name _____

GO AWAY, PLEASE

Charlie's mother left for the dentist's office at 3:30 p.m. Ten minutes later, Charlie was stretched out on the couch in front of the TV, ready to enjoy the sandwich he'd just fixed, when he heard something on the front porch.

"I wonder what that is," thought Charlie. "I think I'll go look out and see."

When he looked out, he saw a stranger trying to turn the doorknob. When the man saw Charlie, he smiled and yelled, "Hey, kid, open the door. I need to use your phone."

"Why?" Charlie yelled back. He didn't like the way the man looked at him and didn't want to let him in.

The man rattled the knob again. "My car broke down. I need to call someone to fix it. Let me in."

On the lines below, tell what you would do if you were Charlie and what you would expect to happen next.

_____

_____

_____

_____

_____

_____

_____

_____

_____

_____

Name _____

THE DOG NEXT DOOR

Mrs. Brennan was terrified of dogs. It did not matter whether they were large or small. She was afraid of them and would not allow her son Grant to have one.

Grant wanted a dog very much. He liked to walk his neighbor's St. Bernard every day after school. He loved the way the big dog licked him and played with him. He was a wonderful animal. Grant promised himself that when he grew up, he would have a big St. Bernard just like Shaggy.

One day when Grant brought Shaggy back after their walk, his neighbor said, "Grant, we are moving to a new apartment that won't allow us to keep a pet. Because you love Shaggy so much and he loves you, we want you to have him for your very own!"

On the lines below, write what you would do if you were Grant and what you would expect to happen next.

_____

_____

_____

_____

_____

_____

_____

_____

_____

_____

Name _____

BAD JOKES ARE NOT FUNNY

Randy is the only part-Indian child in his school. His ancestors were members of the Cherokee tribe, and he is proud of his background. Brent, a troublemaker, makes jokes about Randy and calls him "Big Chief Randy." You are tired of hearing Brent make fun of Randy, and you decide to do something.

Would you...

1. Talk with your teacher about the situation? _____

2. Try to talk with Brent yourself? _____

3. Say something to Randy? _____

Explain your answer. _____

_____

_____

_____

Write a paragraph to tell about a time when someone you know was made fun of and how you think he or she felt.

Name _____

LOCKED OUT!

Henry was home alone and had **strict** instructions not to open the door or leave the house for any reason. Suddenly he heard the doorbell. When he looked out the front window and saw the postman standing there with a big package, he decided he should accept the package. Just as he opened the door and said hello to the postman, his cat dashed out the door and streaked away down the street. Without thinking, Henry slammed the door behind him and ran after the cat. But before he got past the next house, he stopped.

"Oh, no," he groaned, "I've left my key inside. I'm locked out!"

On the lines below, write what you would do if you were Henry and what you would expect to happen next.

_____

_____

_____

_____

_____

_____

_____

_____

_____

_____

_____

_____

Name _____

BORROWED TROUBLE

As Albert rode home on the school bus, he thought about the wonderful time he'd had at the class picnic. There had been lots of food and games, but he'd enjoyed the softball game most of all. Since he'd borrowed his older brother's ball and brought it for everyone to use, the kids let him be a team captain, and his team won! Later his friend Ralph asked Albert if he could borrow the ball and bring it back to him at school the next day. Albert had agreed and was feeling extra good that he had made Ralph happy.

When the bus stopped, Albert got off whistling. As he walked toward his house, he saw his brother and three friends sitting on the front porch. All the boys had bats and gloves and looked like they were waiting for something. Suddenly Albert felt sick. He realized that they were waiting for him to bring the borrowed ball.

On the lines below, write what you would do in that situation, what you would expect to happen next, and how you think Albert's relationship with his brother will be affected.

_____

_____

_____

_____

_____

_____

_____

_____

_____

Name_____

SURPRISE! SURPRISE!

Martha loved to listen to country music. She spent most of her allowance and gift money to buy her favorite compact discs. Since she didn't have her own compact disc player, she used her parents' stereo, but she could use it only one hour a day. More than anything in the world, she wanted her own compact disc player and had hinted to her grandmother that she'd love one for her birthday.

On her birthday, Martha's grandmother came to have dinner with the family. She brought in a big, heavy-looking package. Martha just knew it was her compact disc player!

After dinner and birthday cake, Martha opened her presents, saving her grandmother's package for last. She got lots of nice things and thanked her family. Finally she started on the last package. She ripped off the paper, opened the big brown cardboard box, and saw...a dictionary!

On the lines below, write what you would do in this situation, what you would expect to happen next, and how you think the other people at the party would feel.

_____

_____

_____

_____

_____

_____

_____

_____

_____

Name_____

A SPENDING SPREE

But I Love Them!

Bettina pulled weeds from a neighbor's vegetable garden and walked another neighbor's dog to earn money of her own. While on a shopping trip with a friend, Bettina spent all the money she had earned. She purchased two compact discs, a book, and some purple and green polka-dot knee socks. She rushed home to show her new possessions to her parents.

Bettina's father told her that he didn't approve her buying the compact discs or the book. He said the compact discs would be loud and disturbing to the family and that the book was for adults. Her mother said the purple and green polka-dot socks were ugly, too expensive, and that Bettina would have no place to wear them.

Both parents concluded that Bettina had spent her money unwisely. They asked her to return or exchange the purchases. Bettina replied that she had saved the money and should be allowed to spend it any way she wanted.

What would you do if you were Bettina's parents? _____

_____

_____

_____

What would you do if you were Bettina? _____

_____

_____

How do you think Bettina and her parents could work together to solve the problem? _____

_____

_____

_____

Name _____

ACCIDENTS DO HAPPEN

Karen and David were waiting for the bus and discussing their homework when Karen realized she'd left her notebook in the classroom.

"Oh, no!" she cried. "Here comes the bus!"

"Hurry!" David said. "Go get your notebook. I'll ask the driver to wait."

Karen ran back into the building, down the hall, and into the classroom. She grabbed her notebook, and in her rush to get back to the bus stop, she crashed into the class aquarium. The whole thing shattered. Fish and water went everywhere!

On the lines below, write what you would do if you were Karen and what you think would happen next.

_____

_____

_____

_____

_____

_____

_____

_____

_____

_____

Name _____

TRUTH OR CONSEQUENCES

Clarissa walked very slowly down the hall to Mr. Duncan's room. She'd forgotten to do her homework assignment and didn't know what to do. The other kids were putting their papers on his desk as they walked in. Clarissa went slowly to the desk.

"Oh, Mr. Duncan," she stammered, "I forgot...I forgot to...uh, I forgot to bring my paper. I left it at home."

"That's too bad, Clarissa," said Mr. Duncan. "But it's OK this time. Just bring it in tomorrow, and don't forget again."

Clarissa sat down at her desk feeling worse than before. How could she have lied to Mr. Duncan? He was always so nice and understanding. She wanted to tell him the truth now, but she was afraid.

On the lines below, write what you would do if you were Clarissa and what you would expect to happen next.

_____

_____

_____

_____

_____

_____

_____

_____

_____

_____

Name _____

FRIENDSHIP RATING

Consider each statement carefully before circling the rating that best describes you. Then add up your points and choose your rating.

	3 points	2 points	1 point
1. I listen carefully when my friend talks.	always	sometimes	seldom
2. I try to be sympathetic and help find a solution when my friend has a problem.	always	sometimes	seldom
3. I think of and share ideas for new projects and creative activities.	always	sometimes	seldom
4. I try to be cheerful and cooperative even when I feel grumpy.	always	sometimes	seldom
5. I share my toys and supplies.	always	sometimes	seldom
6. I laugh with but never at my friend.	always	sometimes	seldom
7. I try not to be jealous or possessive when my friend has another friend.	always	sometimes	seldom
8. I am honest with my friend.	always	sometimes	seldom
9. I do not hold grudges.	always	sometimes	seldom
10. I take time to think about what my friend really likes to do.	always	sometimes	seldom
11. I do not tell secrets that my friend tells me.	always	sometimes	seldom
12. I tell my friend when I have a problem or need help.	always	sometimes	seldom
13. I remember my friend's birthday or other special day.	always	sometimes	seldom

Check your rating:
33 to 39 – True Friend
24 to 32 – Good Friend
Below 24 – Improvement needed

Name _____

© 1991 by Incentive Publications, Inc., Nashville, TN.

THE GOOD DEED PYRAMID

A wise man once said, "One good deed deserves another."

Have you ever stopped to think about the good deeds that other people do for you and the good deeds you do for other people?

Who does more good deeds, you or other people?

To help find the answer to this question, fill in each building block in the pyramid below with a good deed that has been done by you or for you in the past few days. Write yours on your side, theirs on their side. Will your pyramid be balanced?

Good deeds done by you   Good deeds done for you

Name _____

READING AHEAD

Every Friday afternoon, Mr. Jordon reads a chapter from an exciting adventure book to the class. Although he likes his students to read whatever they want, he did ask them not to read that particular book since he wanted the class to enjoy it together.

One Wednesday during the free reading period, he noticed that Gregory, who usually read sports magazines, was reading a big, thick book. He walked over and asked Gregory what he was reading. Gregory turned red and showed Mr. Jordan his book. It was the very same adventure book Mr. Jordan read aloud and had asked the students not to read.

Write about the feelings you would have if you were Gregory.

_____

_____

_____

_____

_____

Write about the feelings you would have if you were Mr. Jordan.

_____

_____

_____

_____

Name_____

A TOUGH TEST

Mrs. Bea Tough had taught at Greene School for twenty-two years and was known as a fair but firm teacher. Every Monday Mrs. Bea Tough gave difficult tests. She told her classes that the tests would help them develop self-discipline and good study habits.

Tommy thought Mrs. Bea Tough was a good teacher. She explained math problems well, had a free reading program, and gave good homework assignments. But he did not like the tests on Monday because he had to study each weekend. Tommy asked his classmates to help him write a letter to the principal requesting that Mrs. Bea Tough not give tests on Monday. The other students told Mrs. Bea Tough about Tommy's plan. She asked Tommy to stay after school to talk about the letter.

Write about the feelings you would have if you were Tommy.

_____

_____

_____

_____

Write about the feelings you would have if you were Mrs. Bea Tough.

_____

_____

_____

_____

_____

Name _____

A FAMILY MATTER

Jeanne was twenty pounds overweight. The doctor told her that she must go on a diet at once or she might develop health problems. So her mother carefully replanned the family meals and served foods that Jeanne could eat. She served only fruit for dessert.

After several weeks with Jeanne dieting, Jeanne's brother Ken had a birthday. Their mother decided to make him a birthday cake even though Jeanne couldn't have any. When it was time for dessert, Ken blew out the candles, sliced the cake, and passed it around. Jeanne thought she would get cake, too, but she was given a plate with grapes and an apple on it instead.

Jeanne jumped up and screamed at Ken, "I hate you! I hope you have a terrible birthday!" She ran to her room and locked the door. When Jeanne's mother tried to talk to her, Jeanne screamed through the locked door, "Go away! I hate everyone in this family!"

Write about the feelings you would have if you were Jeanne.

_____

_____

_____

_____

Write about the feelings you would have if you were Jeanne's mother.

_____

_____

_____

_____

Name_____

CHOICES

Reginald and Eva were brother and sister. They both wanted to go to summer camp. Their parents made a deal with them. "We will give you half the money for camp," said their father, "but you must earn the other half by working around the house and yard."

Eva whined that she was too busy with school to work. "You will have plenty of time to work on weekends and after school," said her mother.

Reginald worked hard every day. He mowed the yard, carried groceries, and took out trash. Eva was always busy with friends and never tried to earn any money. When summer came, Reginald started packing his duffel bag for camp. Eva pouted and was mean to her brother. She said it was not fair for their parents to give him camp money when she had to stay home.

Write about the feelings you would have if you were Reginald.

_____

_____

_____

_____

Write about the feelings you would have if you were Eva.

_____

_____

_____

_____

Name _____

A BAD SCENE

Bernie had lived in the little house on Chrome Street as long as he could remember. Even after his parents were divorced three years ago, he and his mom stayed there. Bernie loved the friendly front porch, the comfortable den, and the treehouse that Clark, his mother's boyfriend, helped him build.

One day when Bernie was helping his mom make some stew, she told him that she and Clark were getting married. Bernie was very happy. He liked Clark and enjoyed working and talking with him. Then his mom said that since their house was so small, they were all going to live in Clark's big house across town.

At first Bernie couldn't believe it. Suddenly he began to cry, and he threw the bowl of stew he was holding to the floor. Stew and pieces of china went everywhere. When his mom scolded him and told him to apologize, he ran out of the room yelling, "I won't! I won't go! I won't!"

Write about the feelings you would have if you were Bernie.

_____

_____

_____

_____

Write about the feelings you would have if you were Bernie's mother.

_____

_____

_____

_____

Name _____

THE TROUBLEMAKER

"Jerome," said his dad, "I've just been on the phone with your teacher. Ms. Evans said she's worried about you. Your grades are falling down, you haven't been paying attention in class, and you've been mean to some of the kids. Now what's going on?"

"Aw, Dad," Jerome sighed, "Leonard and I have just been having some fun. He's taught me some real neat things."

"Like locking a girl in the closet and bullying little kids on the playground? I don't think that's so neat. In fact, I don't like it at all. From now on, you are not to play with Leonard, and that's final!"

Write about the feelings you would have if you were Jerome.

_____

_____

_____

_____

_____

Write about the feelings you would have if you were Jerome's dad.

_____

_____

_____

_____

_____

Name _____

POOR PUPPY

Katy got a puppy for her twelfth birthday and named it Garbanzo. Her little brother Ian was jealous because he did not get a present, and his tenth birthday seemed far away. One afternoon Katy came home and went to see Garbanzo. She walked into the playroom and saw Ian throwing toys at the puppy. Garbanzo was huddled in the corner, shaking with fright.

"Ian, you are nasty and cruel!" shouted Katy. She picked up a large fire truck and hit Ian's leg as hard as she could. Their mother ran in and demanded an explanation. Katy said Ian was scaring Garbanzo. Ian cried that he hadn't hurt the dumb dog and was only playing.

Write about the feelings you would have if you were Katy.

_____

_____

_____

_____

_____

Write about the feelings you would have if you were Ian.

_____

_____

_____

_____

_____

Name _____

CONFUSED

Lucy invited her friend Kristy to her house to play. While Kristy was there, Lucy's friend Wendy called to say that she had one extra ticket for the circus! If Lucy could go with them, they would pick her up in ten minutes. Lucy was so excited about going to the circus that she said yes right away. But when she hung up the phone, she suddenly remembered that Kristy was there and that Wendy had only one extra ticket.

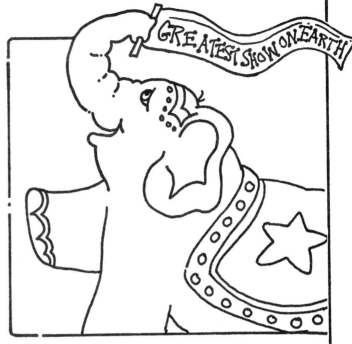

Write about the feelings you would have if you were Lucy.

_____

_____

_____

_____

_____

_____

Write about the feelings you would have if you were Kristy.

_____

_____

_____

_____

_____

_____

Name _____

A CLUBHOUSE QUARREL

Danny and Ronnie lived next door to each other and were best friends. They worked all summer to build a clubhouse. Danny's grandfather gave him some lumber from his workshop and let the boys borrow his tools. Ronnie used his allowance to buy the nails. Since Ronnie had a bigger yard, they built the clubhouse behind his family's house.

At the end of the summer, Danny's family had to move away. Danny wanted to take the clubhouse with him. Ronnie thought the clubhouse should stay in his yard where it was built.

Write about the feelings you would have if you were Danny.

_____
_____
_____
_____
_____

Write about the feelings you would have if you were Ronnie.

_____
_____
_____
_____
_____

Name _____

BACK TO BASICS
IN BUSINESS

Jon and Tony have been friends since kindergarten. This summer they used their savings to build a lemonade stand. They worked hard and made a good bit of money selling lemonade to their friends.

Now that summer is over and school is about to begin again, John wants to sell the lemonade stand and divide the money they have made. Tony wants to move the stand closer to the school and use the money to buy more equipment to add to their business.

Jon likes to play ball, and he wants his share of the money so he can buy a new bat and some special shoes. Tony likes the business and wants to continue to work hard to keep the business going.

Even though the two boys worked together all summer, they are beginning to bicker and argue. Neither of them will agree to the other's point of view.

What will the consequences be if...

1. They sell the lemonade stand to two other boys who will work hard and make it even more successful?

_____

_____

2. They keep the stand and Jon comes to work every day in a bad mood?

_____

_____

3. They close the stand, divide the money, and forget all about the lemonade business?

_____

_____

Can you think of any other solution to the boys' dilemma?

_____

Name_____

GETTING ALONG WITH GROWNUPS

1. One thing the grownups I know do that I especially like is _____ _____ _____ .

2. One thing the grownups I know do that I hate is _____ _____ .

3. One thing I do that the grownups I know especially like is _____ _____ _____ .

4. One thing I do that the grownups I know just hate is _____ _____ .

5. One thing the grownups I know could do to make life easier and more pleasant for kids is _____ _____ .

6. One thing I could do to make life easier and more pleasant for the grownups I know is _____ _____ .

7. One thing I think grownups and kids should talk more about is ___ _____ .

8. One thing I think grownups and kids should do together more often is _____ _____ .

9. One thing I hope I will remember to do for kids when I am grown up is _____ _____ .

Name _____

FAVORITE THINGS

Read the stories below.
Write or draw an ending for each story to show what you think will happen.

Name _____

OH NO!

Read the stories below.
Write or draw an ending for each story to show what you think will happen.

Name _____

MONEY MATTERS

Read the stories below.
Write or draw an ending for each story to show what you think will happen.

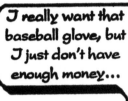

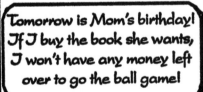

Name _____

FAIR PLAY

Read the stories below.
Write or draw an ending for each story to show what you think will happen.

Name

CONSCIENTIOUS CONCLUSIONS

Read the stories below.
Write or draw an ending for each story to show what you think will happen.

Name _____

STICKY SITUATIONS

Read the stories below.
Write or draw an ending for each story to show what you think will happen.

WHAT NEXT?

Read the stories below.
Write or draw an ending for each story to show what you think will happen.

Name _____

WHICH WOULD YOU RATHER BE?

1000 Friends

1. Would you rather be rich or famous? _____
   Why? _____
   _____
   _____
   _____.

2. Would you rather be beautiful or brilliant? _____
   Why? _____
   _____
   _____.

3. Would you rather be artistic or athletic?_____
   Why? _____
   _____.

4. Would you rather be handsome or talented?_____
   Why? _____
   _____.

5. Would you rather be creative or well-organized? _____
   Why? _____
   _____.

6. Would you rather be a good reader or a good writer? _____
   Why? _____
   _____.

7. Would you rather have a thousand dollars or a thousand friends?
   _____
   Why? _____
   _____.

Name_____

TIME TO BE GRATEFUL

Fill this bag with words or pictures to show twenty things for which you are grateful.

Name_____

PERSONAL CHOICES

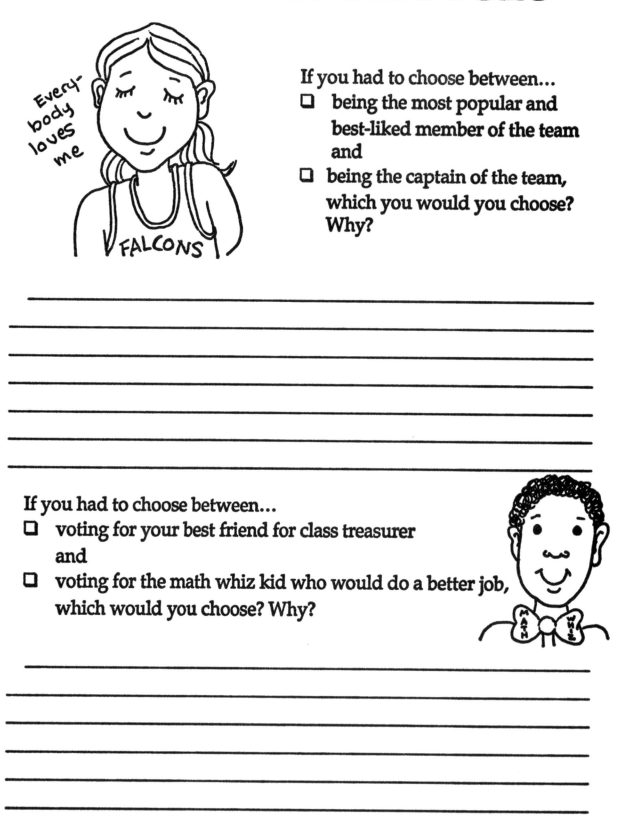

Every-body loves me

FALCONS

If you had to choose between...
- ❑ being the most popular and best-liked member of the team and
- ❑ being the captain of the team, which you would you choose? Why?

_____

_____

_____

_____

_____

_____

_____

_____

If you had to choose between...
- ❑ voting for your best friend for class treasurer and
- ❑ voting for the math whiz kid who would do a better job, which would you choose? Why?

_____

_____

_____

_____

_____

_____

Name_____

POPULARITY POLL

If you had to choose between...

❑ studying to make an A on the geography test
and

❑ studying to learn as much as possible about geography, which one would you choose? Why?

_____

_____

_____

_____

_____

_____

If you had to choose between...

❑ using your lunch money for lunch and

❑ adding it to the class fund for a gift for a classmate in the hospital, which would you choose? Why?

_____

_____

_____

_____

_____

_____

Name _____

FRIENDSHIPS ON THE LINE

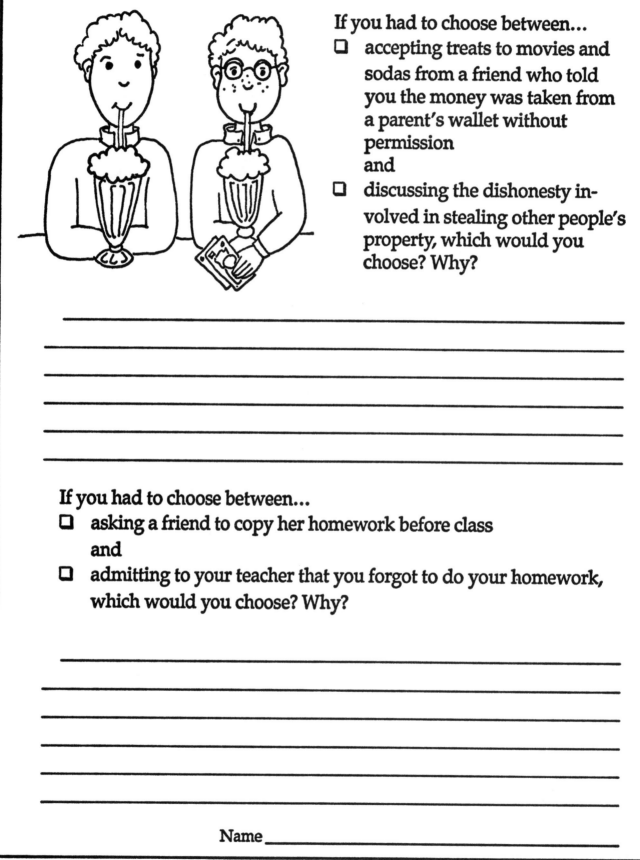

If you had to choose between...
- ❑ accepting treats to movies and sodas from a friend who told you the money was taken from a parent's wallet without permission
  and
- ❑ discussing the dishonesty involved in stealing other people's property, which would you choose? Why?

_____

_____

_____

_____

_____

_____

If you had to choose between...
- ❑ asking a friend to copy her homework before class
  and
- ❑ admitting to your teacher that you forgot to do your homework, which would you choose? Why?

_____

_____

_____

_____

_____

_____

Name _____

TOUGH CHOICES

If you had to choose between...
- ❑ designing and constructing your own science project
and
- ❑ asking your neighbor, whose hobby is science, to do it for you,
which would you choose? Why?

_____

_____

_____

_____

_____

_____

If you had to choose between...
- ❑ telling the librarian that your sister tore some pages from a book you checked out and that you would pay for the book with your own money
and
- ❑ returning the damaged book with no comment, which would you choose? Why?

_____

_____

_____

_____

_____

_____

Name _____

SCHOOL COOL

Check the box that best explains how you think you approach the school day.

Then count the numbers on the boxes you checked to find your "school cool" rating.

A. I arrive on time
   1. ☐ some of the time
   2. ☐ most of the time
   3. ☐ always

B. I have my homework completed
   1. ☐ some of the time
   2. ☐ most of the time
   3. ☐ always done

C. My homework is usually
   1. ☐ carelessly done
   2. ☐ OK
   3. ☐ my very best

D. I obey school rules
   1. ☐ only when I have to
   2. ☐ grudgingly
   3. ☐ cheerfully

E. I contribute ideas and suggestions for classroom projects
   1. ☐ never
   2. ☐ seldom
   3. ☐ often

F. I think my classmates find me to be
   1. ☐ disagreeable
   2. ☐ agreeable
   3. ☐ cheerfully cooperative

H. When I think about school, I
   1. ☐ dread it
   2. ☐ feel it's OK
   3. ☐ look forward to it

Score:
Count the threes.
7 or 8 threes give you a "school cool" rating.
5 or 6 threes give you a "not so school cool" rating.
1 through 5 threes gives you a "no school cool" rating.

Name _____

MY HERO

The person I would like to be just like when I grow up is:

_____

Three things I admire about this person are:

1. _____
2. _____
3. _____

Three things I would like to do if I grow up to be like this person are:

1. _____
2. _____
3. _____

To help me grow up to be like this person, I could begin now to:

1. _____
2. _____
3. _____

Everyone likes to be admired. Maybe I should tell the person I want to be like how I feel.

Name _____

BADGES OF HONOR

BADGE OF COURAGE

BADGE of GENEROSITY

BADGE OF FRIENDSHIP

Write the name of the person you know who is the most deserving of each badge below.

Write just one sentence to tell why you chose this person for the badge of honor.

Name _____

Because _____

_____

_____

_____

Name _____

Because _____

_____

_____

_____

Name _____

Because _____

_____

_____

_____

Name _____

WHAT DO YOU APPRECIATE?

Two, four, six, eight –
What do you appreciate?
- health
- wealth
- fame
- friends
- family
- education
- recreation
- achievement

Your dictionary defines *appreciation* as _____

_____

_____

Think about this definition and select words from the appreciation list above to fill in the blanks.

1. Two years ago, I probably appreciated _____ less than I do now.
2. Four years from now, I expect to appreciate _____ as much as I do now.
3. Six years from now, I will probably appreciate _____ more than I do now.
4. Eight years from now, I will have learned a lot about life. I hope I will appreciate _____ more than I do now.

Write the names of people, places, or things that you *especially* appreciate right now.

1. _____   6. _____

2. _____   7. _____

3. _____   8. _____

4. _____   9. _____

5. _____   10. _____

Name _____

DECISIONS, DECISIONS

If you had to choose between...
- ❑ buying a coat that is not well-made and is of poor-quality fabric but is very much in style this year
  and
- ❑ buying a less stylish coat that will keep you warm and dry, which would you choose? Why?

_____

_____

_____

_____

_____

_____

_____

If you had to choose between...
- ❑ a teacher who gives a lot of homework and enforces all the rules and whose students score well on achievement tests
  and
- ❑ a teacher who is not as strict, gives almost no homework, and makes very few demands on students, which would you choose? Why?

_____

_____

_____

_____

_____

_____

Name _____

IF THE CHOICE WERE YOURS

If you had to choose between...
- ☐ staying home with a cousin who was coming to visit you because his mother was in the hospital
  and
- ☐ going to summer camp as you had planned, which would you choose? Why?

_____

_____

_____

_____

_____

If you had to choose between...
- ☐ telling your mother that you saw your brother break one of her best china teacups
  and
- ☐ letting her think the cat broke it, which would you choose? Why?

_____

_____

_____

_____

_____

Name _____

A MONEY PROBLEM

Elaine has been saving money to buy a special gift for her friend Lynda. Lynda's birthday is next Friday, and Elaine has found the perfect gift in the game store downtown.

The problem is...

Elaine spent $2 of the money to buy a ticket to the hockey game. Now she needs the $2 for Lynda's present.

She could try to sell the hockey ticket to a friend, *but* she really wants to go to the game as it is the last game of the season.

She could look for a less expensive present for Lynda, *but* she and Lynda shop together at the game store, and she knows exactly what Lynda wants.

She could give Lynda a present card with a note telling her the present will be delivered later, *but* she knows how much Lynda is counting on having a present to open at her birthday party.

What would you do if you were Elaine?_____

_____

Why?_____

_____

_____

How would you feel if you were Lynda and Elaine did what you said *you* would do? _____

_____

_____

Why?_____

_____

_____

Name_____

FOR OUTSTANDING SERVICE

Fill out this Outstanding Service Award and present it to a person who, in your opinion, has contributed greatly to making your home, classroom, or community a better place to be. Be sure to give the reason for your choice.

Outstanding
Service Award

Presented to _____
(name)

on_____
(date)

Because _____

_____

_____

_____

_____

_____

_____

_____
(Signature)

Name _____

PERSONALITY PARADE

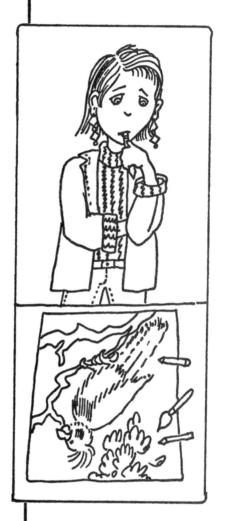

Tammy likes to sing and dance and tell stories. She has a good imagination and is always cheerful. Sometimes she forgets her lunch money or library books, and she often forgets to do her homework.

Tommy is strong, well-coordinated, and very good at sports. He is quiet and keeps his thoughts to himself. He does not like reading or geography, but he does well in math and science.

David is generous, kind, and loves to do things for people. He has a good sense of humor and loves to make people laugh. Grownups like David a lot, and some kids say he is the teacher's pet.

Myra is a sad girl who needs to be cheered up by her classmates. She worries about her studies and often does not finish her work. Myra is a creative girl. She always wins art contests and writes very good poetry. She likes to work alone and "do her own thing" rather than be part of a group.

Which of these people would you choose for your best friend? _____

_____

Why?_____

Which of these people would you choose to sit beside in the classroom?

Why?_____

Which of these people would you choose to be most like? _____

Why? _____

Which of these people do you think would be most likely to win a class popularity contest?_____

Why?_____

Name _____

GIVE YOUR REASON

Circle a choice for each situation. Then explain your choice.

Situation	You choose to:

1. You think a school rule is very unfair.

   (a) talk to the teacher about the rule
   (b) talk to the other kids about the rule
   (c) do nothing

Reason for the choice: _____

_____

_____

2. Your teacher asks you to tell who wrote undesirable words on the wall.

   (a) tell who did it
   (b) ask the kid who did it to confess
   (c) do neither of the above

Reason for the choice: _____

_____

_____

_____

3. A good friend has told a secret that you asked him not to tell.

   (a) refuse to talk to your friend
   (b) tell the friend how angry you are
   (c) tell someone else how angry you are

Reason for the choice:_____

_____

_____

_____

Name _____

TOUCHING CHOICES

We make many choices every day.

Some of the choices we make affect only our lives. Other choices affect the lives of other people.

Think of three choices that you have made in the past week that may have affected the life of another person. Write two sentences that tell how you think your choice affected the person.

Choice	Effect
1. _____	_____ _____ _____ _____
2. _____	_____ _____ _____ _____
3. _____	_____ _____ _____ _____

Name _____

PERSONALLY SPEAKING

The person in my class whom I would choose as a lifelong friend is

_____.

Three reasons why I would choose this person are:

1. _____
2. _____
3. _____

If I had to spend a month on a desert island with only one person, the person I would choose is _____.

Three reasons why I would choose this person are:

1. _____
2. _____
3. _____

The person I would choose to live next door to for the next five years is_____.

Three reasons why I would choose this person are:

1. _____
2. _____
3. _____

Name _____

ONE WORLD

Read each statement below and check **true** or **false** to tell how you feel about the statement. Then write **one sentence** to give the reason for your choice.

	True	False
1. People from all over the world should share their natural resources with each other.	☐	☐

_____

_____

| 2. The leaders of the countries of the world share and work together better now than they did ten years ago. | ☐ | ☐ |

_____

_____

| 3. When I am grown up, we will be closer to world peace than we are now. | ☐ | ☐ |

_____

_____

| 4. Young people can contribute to world understanding by trying to learn more about the customs and beliefs of young people in other countries. | ☐ | ☐ |

_____

_____

| 5. People in other countries feel that people in our country are working toward world peace and understanding. | ☐ | ☐ |

_____

_____

Name_____

THE ME I'M LEARNING TO BE

Use words and pictures to design a "Me" poster to show the world what you are really like. Think about your family, friends, school, organizations, country, community, books, hobbies, talents, sports, and anything that is important to you. Even you may be surprised!

Name _____